In the Footprints *of* Loneliness

In the Footprints of Loneliness

Meditations—
when you hear an echo in your heart

Catherine de Hueck Doherty

MADONNA HOUSE PUBLICATIONS
Combermere, Ontario, Canada

Madonna House Publications®
2888 Dafoe Rd, RR 2
Combermere ON K0J 1L0

www.madonnahouse.org/publications

First Edition

Third Printing, August 2017

Second printing, December 21st, 2009.

Printed in Canada

Scripture quotations are taken from the New Jerusalem Bible, copyright © 1985 by Darton, Longman & Todd, London, and Doubleday, a division of Random House, Inc., New York.

Edited by Martin Nagy. Parts of this work previously appeared in the book *Doubts, Loneliness, Rejection* by Catherine Doherty, which was published by Madonna House Publications in 1993.

National Library of Canada Cataloguing in Publication Data
Doherty, Catherine de Hueck (née Kolyschkine), 1896–1985
   In the footprints of loneliness : meditations—when you hear an echo in your heart / Catherine de Hueck Doherty.

ISBN 978-0-921440-90-1

   1. Meditations. 2. Spiritual life–Catholic authors. I. Title.

BT771.3.D628 2003   242   C2003-904427-0

Design by Rob Huston

This book is set in Berkeley Oldstyle, designed by Frederick W. Goudy for the University of California Press in 1938. Headings are set in Balzano, designed by America's famous carver of inscriptions, John Benson.

From that place, you can see the pain of mankind. Not only see it, but share it.
Above all other pains in this age...is the pain of loneliness. Loneliness walks with everyone.

Catherine Doherty, *Uródivoi*

But look, I am going to seduce her
and lead her into the desert
and speak to her heart.

Hosea 2:16

Contents

Foreword

Catherine Doherty was fond of St. Silouhan's life and sayings. He was a Russian monk who lived on the Holy Mountain. He counseled his spiritual children, "Fold your mind into your heart," and "Keep your heart in hell and do not despair."

"Keep your heart in hell and do not despair": this is life with Christ, for Christ came to save sinners. Hell is our separation from God. In this sense, walking in loneliness is a walk through hell. But Christ has not abandoned us. He does not forsake us in this hell. He came to walk with us and to save us from hell. We create *our own* loneliness through sin. God creates *his* loneliness in us to keep us longing for and returning to him; God gives us a share in his loneliness by drawing each of us into the garden and onto the cross with Christ.

If we walk with Christ, if we love Christ, we find ourselves hanging with the crucified Christ, who out of his love for humanity, out of his love for sinners went to the Garden of Gethsemane and all alone walked with every sinner, and took each and every sin with him to the cross. If you love Christ, if you enter his heart, then, you will find yourself in the loneliness of the garden, in the loneliness of all humanity. If you want to stay close to the heart of Christ, then you have to go to where Jesus is—on the cross. As Catherine often intimated, Christ left the other side of his cross open for you, so that you could hang there with him, close to his heart, for the sake of the world, loving all sinners, making your loneliness—Christ's loneliness—a prayer for all people.

In Jesus' Sacred Heart, your own loneliness becomes a prayer, your life becomes a prayer, you become a prayer. You do not despair, because Jesus is with you, the fire in your heart, your Beloved.

After more than fifty years as a monk, Archmandrite Sophrony, one of St. Silouhan's spiritual children, wrote:

"Prayer is delight for the spirit. But the circumstances accompanying this creative work are complex. Time after time we experience an eager upsurge towards God, followed repeatedly by a falling away from His Light. Time and again we are conscious of the mind's inability to rise to Him. There are moments when we feel ourselves on the verge of madness. Pain forces the cry, 'Thou didst give me Thy precept to love, which I accept with all my being, but there is no strength in me for this love. Thou Who art love, come and abide in me, and perform in me all that Thou hast enjoined, for Thy commandment exceeds my powers. My mind is too frail to comprehend Thee. My spirit cannot see into the mysteries of Thy life. I desire to do Thy will in all things but my days go by in perpetual conflict. I am tortured by the fear of losing Thee because of the evil thoughts in my heart; and this fear crucifies me. I sink. Lord, save me, as Thou didst save Peter who dared to walk on the water, to go to Thee.'

"At times prayer seems over-slow in bringing results, and life is so short. Instinctively we cry, 'Make haste unto me.' But He does not always respond at once. Like fruit on a tree, our soul is left to scorch in the sun, to endure the cold wind, the scorching wind, to die of thirst or be drowned in the rain. But if we do not let go of the hem of His garment, all will end well.

"Prayer assuredly revives in us the divine breath which God breathed into Adam's nostrils…But again and again I find myself reflecting that life is full of paradox, like all the Gospel teaching. 'I am come to send fire on the earth; and what will I, if it be already kindled?' All we sons of Adam must go though this heavenly flame that consumes our deathly passions. Otherwise we shall not see the fire transformed into the light of new life, for it is not light that comes first, and then fire: in our fallen state burning must precede enlightenment. Let us therefore, bless the Lord for the consuming action of His love…There is no other way for us mortals to become 'children of the resurrection,' children of God, to reign together with Christ, the only-begotten Son of God. However painful this re-creating may be however it may distress and lacerate—the process, agonizing as it is, in the end will be a blessed one."[1]

Catherine Doherty lived with the fire of her Beloved in her own heart. She knew the loneliness of being human. She knew man's loneliness and heard God's loneliness echo in her heart. Pray through Catherine's meditations. She offers these experiences of her life with God as a guide to her fellow pilgrims. Find for yourself consolation, prayer, and fortitude to walk through your own loneliness and follow in the footprints of your Beloved.

Martin Nagy, Editor
Feast of the Presentation of Mary, 2002

---

1   *On Prayer,* Archmandrite Sophrony, trans. from Russian by Rosemary Edmonds, © 1996 by Patriarchal Stavropegic Monastery of St John the Baptist, Tolleshunt Knights by Maldon, Essex. St. Vladimir's Seminary Press, New York.

Introduction

The greatest pain of the world today is loneliness and the feeling that we are not loved.

Loneliness becomes like a monster that drives a person somewhere—anywhere—anywhere. Sometimes it is like a thousand switches that drive you to run. That's why so many people go from Timbuktu to India—from India to Alaska—from Alaska to Russia, and so forth, and back again. It's loneliness. Sometimes we daydream. That's dangerous. To imagine this and that and the other thing that will never happen, takes us deeper and deeper into a personal loneliness that nobody can share, because it isn't reality, but unreality. To accept life as God gives it to us, minute by minute, hour by hour, day by day, to take the duty of the moment very seriously, because it's the will of God, assuages loneliness.

Have you ever considered loneliness a gift of God? We all suffer from loneliness one way or another. The Lord has made this loneliness. We're lonely because we're separated from God. "My heart will not rest," said St. Augustine, "until it rests in Thee." The

Psalmist says, "I desire to see your face more than a hart desires to drink the water."[2]

All the terrible loneliness that is on our backs, that surrounds us, that makes us do strange things, that, like a whip, sends us across worlds to find a release, is simply the loneliness of man for God. It can be assuaged by standing still and allowing God to come close to you. Loneliness will teach you a lot of things. And, above all, it will teach you how much God loves you.

In the depths of every heart, so the scriptures say, there is a garden enclosed. When loneliness comes upon you, when you want to go and hide in some corner, when self-pity carries you like a big, huge wave on a beach all full of stones, and you see that beach in your mind and you think you are going to be broken up, close your eyes and repeat, "In my heart there is a garden enclosed." This enclosure is for God. If you go into that garden, you will hear the incredible sounds that seemingly only one man heard before, and that is the heartbeats of God.

---

2   "As a deer yearns for running streams, so I yearn for you my God." (Psalm 42:1)

For if there was ever a lonely person on earth, it was Jesus Christ. The very essence of his loneliness was in the Garden of Gethsemane, when his beloved apostles slept: "Jesus came with them to a plot of land called Gethsemane…He said to them, 'My soul is sorrowful to the point of death. Wait here and stay awake with me.'… He came back to the disciples and found them sleeping, and he said to Peter, 'So you had not the strength to stay awake with me for one hour?' " (Matthew 26:36–40)

The loneliness of God is given to man, so that man might arise and seek God. Because, when I share the loneliness of the Garden of Gethsemane, of the crucifixion—at that moment, I take upon myself the cross of mankind. I lift the loneliness of all mankind, each one separately, even as Christ did.

You stand alone, abandoned, as far as men are concerned, but loneliness has a strange and quiet face, if you only look at it instead of running away from it into various beds, sex, wrong friendships, the bottle, the drugs. Then, loneliness becomes sort of ugly, a distorted affair. We do not have to go through life desiring to be loved. We must go through life, loving. That is the whole secret.

It's by experiencing loneliness that we know love.

Those of us who try to really love as God asks us to love, must walk that inward journey with our brothers and sisters—no matter how hard, how difficult, how sad, the road may be. We stagger under the weight, but if we believe—if our faith is as deep as it should be—we will carry on.

To console and to be compassionate, though, means almost self-annihilation, it means being eaten up, it means giving yourself to other people. That means I lose myself, I don't think of myself any more. I think of everybody but myself. But who wants to put his hands out, and his feet—and say, "Here I am, Lord. I want to be nailed on the other side of your cross, because I love you". If we did that, we would know happiness, because the cross is the marriage bed of Christ.

In order to learn this, we have to do violence to ourselves. In the Bible, it says, "Heaven is taken by violence"—violence to *me*. Because if you've got the guts to open your heart, and really let people in, then you will be very tired. In fact, lay people, especially, are exceedingly tired, all over the world.

At what point will we understand that happiness lies in entering loneliness, in entering its belly and, there, suddenly meeting God? His way is terrible and harsh. If you don't accept that, you will never know him, and you will never know happiness. If you meet God in loneliness, he will reveal himself to you. And, as soon as I forget myself, the Lord fills me with a consolation that I can give to others, and he gives me compassion for others.

But for that, you have to pray. You have to pray constantly. Remember God in your life, and you will be able to begin to console, to be compassionate.

Bombs explode here, and bombs explode there, and everybody is terrorized, and so forth. How can you live with tensions like that? So, this is the hour of consolation, and of compassion. And we'd better give it. We give it to others, and they'll give it to us. And in that exchange of consolation, compassion, and love, we shall become brothers of Christ, and children of his Father.

Can you imagine the loneliness of Jesus Christ? When He was 12 years of age, his mother and Joseph did not understand what was going on when he was in the temple. He said, "Don't you know that I have to be about my Father's business?" He must have been lonely walking down to Nazareth.

He said to Philip, "Philip, Philip, three years you have walked with me, and you still don't understand." A terrible loneliness must have overshadowed him when his apostles did not understand.

After he resurrected, Thomas said, "Unless I put my finger into his wounds…" God bless Thomas, because it brought forth from Christ, "Blessed are those who have not seen and have believed."

The loneliness of Christ on the cross, you've heard it, "Abba, Abba, why hast Thou forsaken me?" This is the cry of mankind. "Lord hear my prayer, listen to the voice of my supplication. Out of the depths I cry to Thee." That's the cry of faith—naked faith in loneliness. And faith has to be naked. Loneliness makes it naked. It takes away garment by garment, until we follow naked, the naked Christ. For he was naked on the cross—he didn't have anything around his middle.

Our Mandate says, "Be hidden, be a light to your neighbour's feet. Go without fear into the depths of men's hearts. I shall be with you." Why can't I go into the loneliness of another when I love him? A thousand human beings walk around and about us, in the hell of their loneliness, because we are too occupied with ourselves.

I think that God has created loneliness in us so that we might seek—beyond our friends, husbands, wives, even beyond our communities—to really enter into his real plan for us. By becoming one with the Trinity, which is the first community, we become one with all humanity.

In Russia and in the Eastern Rite, a person deliberately seeks loneliness of this type. He seeks it beyond all loneliness accepted in this part of the world. He seeks it for Christ's sake. He has one thought in view—that Christ was lonely and that Christ was pushed around, whipped, slapped, and that people who are pushed around, whipped and slapped are lonely.

When you enter the poustinia[3], that kind of solitude becomes a zeal for your Father's

3 "Poustinia" is the Russian word for "desert."
A poustinia is a place you go to be alone with God in solitude, fasting, and prayer.

house. "Zeal" is really another word for "fire." You start a fire when you are very, very cold; the fire is very slow in burning, and you blow on it, or you have bellows to make it greater. When you are filled with this strange, incredible fire that desires only one thing, to love beyond all your ability to love him, you implore him to increase that ability, and then you grow a fantastic, incredible desire to show God to others, so that they may love him, because therein lies their happiness. It is the solitude of waiting for the fire within oneself to really catch on. It is the solitude of hunger to make the Beloved known by everybody else. There are a thousand solitudes when they are connected with God.

It is in this deep solitude that one waits and loneliness envelops us. There and other places. But it is a creative loneliness. It is a salvific loneliness. It is my loneliness being permitted to share the loneliness of Christ.

The poustinik's[4] loneliness is salvific and of cosmic proportions. The poustinik, in prayer, crosses the universe. When you pray, you cross the universe. This is his contribu-

---

4   A "poustinik" is a person in a poustinia.

tion, by hanging on his cross of loneliness, his healing rays, like the rays of the sun, will penetrate the earth.

The world is cold; someone must be on fire, so that people can come and put their cold hands and feet against that fire. If anyone allows this to happen, then he becomes a fire-place where men can warm themselves. Real zeal is standing still and letting God be a bonfire in you. It is not easy to have God's fire within you. We must have God contribute through us, which means nakedness before him must come first.

You have to pray that immense prayer of silence in which eventually you become a prayer yourself.

Loneliness is a Midwife to Creativity

"My dear friends, do not be taken aback at the testing by fire which is taking place among you, as though something strange were happening to you; but in so far as you share in the sufferings of Christ, be glad, so that you may enjoy a much greater gladness when his glory is revealed…So even those whom God allows to suffer should commit themselves to a Creator who is trustworthy, and go on doing good."

1 Peter 4:12–13, 19

The Hunger for God

There are two kinds of loneliness—the loneliness of God and the loneliness of man.

God put loneliness in our heart so that we would hunger for him. St. Augustine expressed it well: "My heart will not rest until it rests in Thee."

The loneliness of God is God's way of making us grow in faith so as to follow him and find him even before we die. But there is more to it than that—following God, seeking him, following the path of loneliness. That is the path of faith for faith is loneliness. If it weren't lonely it would not be faith. You walk in darkness. You don't know where you are going. You just believe God is leading you so you go.

In Faith and Darkness, God Opens the Talents He Has Given You

Within God's loneliness is hidden creativeness. When I walk in faith and darkness in search of God, God opens in me the talents he has given to me.

All of us have talents. But they lie fallow, because we are usually concentrating on man's loneliness. This could be equal to self-pity, concentrating on "Poor me. I am all alone. No one loves me. I cannot share anything with anybody. Even my wife or husband doesn't understand. My children have left me. I have no one to talk to (not meaning just 'fluffy talk')." True. All true, but there must be no self-pity. If we follow God's call there is always someone there around the corner for us. Self-pity comes from concentrating on man's loneliness rather than the loneliness God has placed in us himself.

The path is narrow, the path is hard, but suddenly you hear the voice say, "Come on. Come on higher. Come on. I love you. I called you. *Listen.*"

So you move another hundred yards maybe, and sometimes no more than a yard, but if you continue and your life is a life of faith, which is a life of loneliness, God begins to show you that loneliness is creative.

God brings forth a talent. It might be woodcarving. It might be pottery. It might be calligraphy writing. It might be any kind of writing.

Or it might be none of these. It might be the greatest of all abilities, to so live in the darkness of faith that you create an atmosphere by saying "yes" to God again and again, and in that atmosphere which is created by God and you, to bring people to God.

In a sense, to be able to create an atmosphere where people are renewed is of God and man. It is a deep and profound thing. In a sense, we create a new heart in those who have lost their heart or think they have—in those who have lost faith, those who have lost goals, those who are full of doubt.

You make up the sufferings that are wanting in Christ. There are no sufferings wanting in Christ, but he makes us co-creator with himself.

Concentrate on God's loneliness. Suffer with Christ. Turn from self-pity toward creativeness. Let your loneliness give birth to and inspire a talent. Offer your talent as a prayer. Do small things exceedingly well for love of God.

Share Your Loneliness with Christ

"God, you are my God, I pine for you;
my heart thirsts for you,
my body longs for you,
as a land parched, dreary and waterless.
Thus I have gazed on you in the sanctuary,
seeing your power and your glory.
Better your faithful love than life itself;
my lips will praise you.
Thus I will bless you all my life,
in your name lift up my hands.
All my longings fulfilled as with fat and rich foods,
a song of joy on my lips and praise in my mouth…
In the shadow of your wings I rejoice."

Psalm 63:1–5, 7

Loneliness Makes Everyone Your Brother or Sister

If we really understood loneliness, we would know without knowing, we would grasp without grasping, we would feel without feeling, just one thing: that my brother is Christ.

This will come to us after awhile. Perhaps one has to go through the poustinia, because in the great desert one can see so clearly the face of God. And in *sobornost*—which is the unity of the Trinity with me and you—it is obvious that he who sees the Father knows the Son, and that only the Son can teach us the Father. He who knows the Son knows mankind, irrespective of nationality, color, locale. All men become brothers of him who is my brother.

The third person of the Trinity, the Holy Spirit, the Crimson Dove, as the Russians say, with his immense third person crimson wings, removes all misunderstanding, all darkness. Now in deed and truth, my brother—the yellow, the red, the black, the white person—becomes Christ. A very strange thing happens. Truly my brother changes into Christ, but what is much more important, Christ becomes my brother. Do you see how everyone who understands this mystery—God teaches it to you—suddenly realizes that the most Holy Trinity surrounds him on all sides?

Then, something happens to loneliness. It ceases to be an illness that I go to the psychiatrist to cure. Why don't you look at your hands and see if perhaps you have in your hands a key? It is a key, a very simple, ordinary key that opens to you the true essence of loneliness, which is *sharing it with Christ*. But if you share it with him, may I ask you, how is it possible to be lonely when you have the key to his loneliness, and the two lonelinesses blend together? Each ceases to be a loneliness.

Celebrate Your Loneliness

You might be in Gethsemane where he was so very lonely. Or you might be anywhere— on a streetcar or a bus, in Ottawa or Paris or Berlin, on some path leading to a rural area. You can share his loneliness at any time, and he will share yours. The result will be that there will not be any loneliness, because when you have entered into the mystery of Christ's loneliness, it ceases to be loneliness.

Out of your soul, out of your mind, out of your heart, comes your dance, and your song, and your joy; for fundamentally, dear friends, our entry into the loneliness of Christ is a time of celebration because we have been given the key to one of the greatest mysteries of God.

It will take you time to slowly bring your hands together. When you are lonely, you sort of look down, and your hands, too, hang down at your sides. But very slowly, as you pray, notwithstanding the drooping arms, notwithstanding the head that seems too heavy for you to carry, notwithstanding the back that is breaking under what you think is his cross, slowly, with a deep breath, your hands come together. First, praying hands, then open hands, lifted up to God as if they were a chalice. You can drink water out of your cupped hands. So you lift them, one next to another.

If you continue to pray, a strange sound will enter your ears and a key will drop into your hands lifted like a chalice to him. Slowly you will take the key, and it will open his heart. You will step over the threshold. He only allows us to see the fringe of his mysteries. There are very few who go into the depth of his mysteries. No doubt, our Lady did.

Using the key, you walk into this mystery. How straight is your back, how raised is your head, and how joyous is your song and dance before him!

Hold hands with him, and go skipping and hopping and jumping with God. Why? Because he has given you the one thing that we all desire but very seldom like to receive—Love. It is painful. It takes much prayer and much wandering across unknown places and deserts and hills. It takes much to love your brother and sister, and therefore, to love your God.

"Eternal Father, open your gates today to the most miserable of your children, but one who greatly longs to see you."

St. Jeanne Jugan

The Loneliness of Being Human

He said to them, "My soul is sorrowful to the point of death. Wait here and stay awake with me." And going on a little further he fell on his face and prayed. "My Father," he said, "If it is possible, let this cup pass me by. Nevertheless, let it be as you, not I, would have it." He came back to the disciples and found them sleeping, and he said to Peter, "So you had not the strength to stay awake with me for one hour? Stay awake, and pray not to be put to the test. The spirit is willing enough, but human nature is weak."

Matthew 26:38–41

The Loneliness of the Incarnation

He has allowed you to penetrate the mystery of his own mystery of loneliness.

Can anyone probe mysteries? We walk on the periphery of that mystery, but we cannot enter it—unless God permits us to. Sometimes he does, and when he does, hold it in your cupped hands.

Have you ever considered how lonely Christ was? What he felt as he entered the womb of his creature? A fantastic loneliness overcame a fetus. Can you, for one second, understand the immense, infinite, the absolutely incredible love of the Father, Son, and Holy Spirit? This is the first of the mysteries. It is not only a love letter that God has written to you and to me, but it is an explosion of love.

We read today of volcanoes which explode. We worry about the explosion of nuclear weapons. But here within your heart, if you let it be open, is the greatest explosion of all—the explosion of the love of God for humans, which goes to the length of becoming a seed in the womb of a woman. Can we understand that fully?

One thing we can do: we can fall on our knees and prostrate ourselves before the incredible mystery of his love. We can continue to meditate on the mysteries, for they are there to be meditated on, as in the Rosary. You hold it in your hand and you move one bead to another bead. It is the love of God for you and me. As you keep passing those beads through your fingers, they become more than beads. They are something very real because they deal with his mysteries.

The Eclipse of God in Our Hearts

In a book that I have written called *Sobornost,* I attempted to describe the unity of God and man. God looked at what he had created, and he decided that he would make man like unto himself. God wanted communication with man, but man did not want to have any communication with God once he had understood the rules of communication. And those rules were rules of love: first the love of God, secondly, people, but man wanted to love himself. So, the apple of pride became bigger and bigger, and appeared like a little moon somewhere in the sky. Only it wasn't in the sky, it was in the heart of men—in your heart and my heart.

We didn't want to communicate with God. It was too hard. Communication with God meant following the second person of the Most Holy Trinity. It meant a sort of station of the cross. When we heard the sound of nails on flesh, we immediately said to ourselves in the darkness of the night, "Not me, God, not me. I'll take some of it, but not all of it." But with God, if we don't take all of it, he disappears.

The Loneliness from Heaven

The loneliness of the unbeliever comes out of hell and not out of heaven. It takes charge of one. All I can do for whoever you are who reads this book, is pray for you.

The loneliness that comes to you from heaven is the loneliness of the Garden of the Gethsemane. The apostles are asleep, but you are not. You touch the rim of another mystery, the mystery of Christ's blood falling on a stone and his cry in the night to his Father. You are next to him. You are part of that mystery of his loneliness, and because you are part of it, your heart begins to burn with a love that you cannot contain. You forget everything, and wordlessly you begin to communicate with him. Then, the loneliness vanishes. You are there, at the crucifixion—and you do not even feel the nails in your hands and feet because love fills your whole person. You are taken out of yourself and you are placed into his heart. You know the price that he paid for you and me. You know it totally and completely.

He is taken off the cross. But in three days, he will appear to many people. In other words, his resurrection is yours. He resurrected for you and for me. You feel the effect of the resurrection in yourself. Deep down, the mystery of it is all around you. Suddenly, you understand. Like St. Paul, like all the apostles, you cannot contain yourself any more.

You have to have contact with everyone—face-to-face, soul-to-soul, mind-to-mind. You begin to touch your brothers and sisters in the world, whoever they are, whether prostitutes or kings. For each of you has a gift. You can give to each the gift of prayer, which is the golden key that God gave you to enter his mysteries.

The greatest mystery of all is: in communicating with God in depth, you communicate with people in depth. Suddenly, because your eyes have been opened, you know that each person that you communicate with is Christ himself. With his arms wide open, he says, "Come to me, all who labour and are overburdened, and I will give you rest."

Friendship and Forgiveness

Then Peter went up to him and said, "Lord how often must I forgive my brother if he wrongs me? As often as seven times?" Jesus answered, "Not seven, I tell you, but seventy-seven times…. Forgive your brother from your heart."

Matthew 18:21–22,35

Cross the Bridge Loneliness Built

Loneliness has built a bridge. To everyone who wants to cross it, loneliness is promised to disappear. When it has not quite disappeared, it has a smiling face. The bridge that, in fact, dispels loneliness is friendship and forgiveness.

I cannot be lonely, I can never be lonely, if I forgive. But forgiveness must be total. Man is not capable of totally forgiving, unless he has recourse to God, and it is only through God, and through the grace of God, that we can forgive one another totally.

Now forgiveness of this type is truly love. It penetrates that mystery that God has given us. He said, "Love one another, as I have loved you." He also added, "Love your enemies." Now then, see how forgiveness dispels loneliness.

It is a bridge that is soon left behind, because once you enter loneliness with a heart full of forgiveness toward those who have hurt you, loneliness disappears. It just isn't there. It can't be there. It flies from forgiveness. Forgiveness is the only remedy that can make loneliness disappear.

Give Everything to Your Brother or Sister

Forgiveness and friendship—as I forgive my brothers and sisters, a new bridge arises. It might be a suspension bridge, it might be one of cement, it doesn't matter. It is a bridge of friendship.

Since you have forgiven your brothers and sisters, you can become friends with them. To be a friend means to share. It is impossible for loneliness to exist between those who share their thoughts and their actions on the basis of forgiveness and friendship.

But friendship, like forgiveness, must be total. It is a strange thing that, as you approach a mystery of Christ, and even as you stand on the periphery of it, a great light dawns on you. You understand without understanding that Christ demands totality. He really does. He would not give one dollar if he had a hundred. And you, also, have to give totally. Our gifts are ours to give freely. Friendship and forgiveness—they must be total. I cannot turn to you and say, "You are my friend," and yet, hide things from you. I must share.

For you see, all of this together becomes a chalice made by the hands of humans for God. That chalice must be pure, and its content must be pure. Friendship must be pure, forgiveness must be pure, and total.

Another thing you must understand if you want to break loneliness is that the totality has to continue until you die. Say that you have made friends with some people and suddenly the shadow of anger, or of unforgiveness, darts through your soul. You haven't done anything to those people except that you have withdrawn. Now, the loneliness that men are afraid of will come and envelop you in its mantle again.

Give Everything to God

You must understand, as I have tried already to explain, that there is a type of loneliness that has nothing to do with friendship or forgiveness. You will always have one type of loneliness, because your heart will never be satisfied unless it is placed into the heart of God. He reserves this joy for himself.

Even though forgiveness, friendship, understanding, and love constantly bind us to one another and present to God a joyful picture, nevertheless, in both the dark of the night and in the noonday sun, I turn my face to him and I say, "Lord, notwithstanding all this you have given me, I am still lonely, because, as of yet, I do not possess you totally."

In a certain sense, then, you will have to remain lonely. But let me tell you, this kind of loneliness is beautiful. It can be likened to the loneliness of a young girl desirous to meet her fiancé. You might be very old, your face wrinkled with age, and your hair gray or white. You might have old shoes or slippers on your feet. You might go with a bag gathering the garbage of others, or you might be wealthy. None of this matters. Whoever you are—man, woman, youth—somehow or other you must think of yourself as lifting your hands toward someone and saying, "Oh, I am lonely, because you are not here."

Whoever you are, see yourself lifting your hands toward someone, toward your brothers and sisters, toward God and saying, "Oh, I am lonely, because you are not here."

"How is it that when there is so little time to enjoy your presence you hide from me?"
St. Teresa of Avila

A Remedy for Loneliness

"I was hungry and you gave me food, I was thirsty and you gave me drink, I was a stranger and you made me welcome, lacking clothes and you clothed me, sick and you visited me, in prison and you came to see me…In truth I tell you, in so far as you did this to one of the least of these brothers of mine, you did it to me."

Matthew 25:35–36, 40

Love God

The first remedy for loneliness is contact with God. That is to say, not only a contact but an incarnation into the Lord. This incarnation is found when two people love one another.

It is obvious that God has passionately loved us, or he would not have died on the cross. The question remains, do we passionately love him? It is not enough to just be in contact with God. There is still a great difference between simple contact with God and being passionately in love with him in such a manner that the gospel and all his words become our guidelines. These are the only guidelines that we acknowledge, because love is like that. Those who love one another march to one tune and no other.

Embrace the Deep Silence of Love

Once this love affair between God and us, and especially between the Second Person and us has been established, God will be there to help us, to confront us. We must have a real confrontation with God. He strips us bare. There is nothing left of us except the naked soul, totally open to God. He can throw away the keys to such a soul, because the doors are open most of the time. This is because everyone who walks into such a soul, into such a heart, is the Lord, is Christ.

Mother Teresa of Calcutta understood that, and in a book entitled *Something Beautiful for God*, Malcolm Muggeridge writes about it. But, it is one thing to write about someone, and it is another thing to experience what that someone lives. I have not met Mother Teresa. I have only corresponded with her. But I think that she and I know each other because we are both in love with God in a deep way. It is hard to describe this state of loving God, for all words become useless.

In a book I wrote entitled *Molchanie*—which means "silence" in Russian—I tried to explain that when one enters the mystery of God, the first mystery is silence. When one loves another, silence is absolutely necessary.

Long before lovers can speak openly of their love, they speak by silence, a deep silence, especially when it deals with God. It is by entering the mystery of silence that slowly everyone becomes like our Beloved. That is true of Mother Teresa. Hers was a very heroic quality. Once that mystery is embraced no words are needed to describe heroism, sanctity, or things of that nature. For everything that we do for the other, my brothers and sisters, is done for him.

Can you really imagine joy, pure unadulterated joy? Well, cup your hands and let joy become bread and wine in your hands. Open your mouth, take it, and swallow it. Receive communion. Become one with God, and at that very moment a very great mystery takes place. In this communion, you will see each face of your brothers and sisters as the face of God.

Set the World on Fire

"Our God is a consuming fire."

Hebrews 12:29

Touch a Stone

Loneliness is a state, an emotion that can come from the depths of hell or from the heights of heaven.

One of the first things in facing loneliness, any kind of loneliness, but especially old age loneliness, is to understand that Christ calls some people to share his loneliness. Then we, too, with his help, can redeem the world. All those who follow in his footsteps, all those who never deviate from his teachings, find that these teachings are revolutionary.

However, no typical revolutionary wants to accept them. Typical revolutionaries want to do what they want to do, when they want to do it, and as they want to do it, but they do not want to do what Christ told them to do. Hence, there is no peace in the world. But those who follow Christ will find peace. They will understand that loneliness is fruitful and not sterile, because we can share it, if we wish to, with God.

A psychiatrist friend used to tell me that whenever people came to ask my advice about loneliness, I should take them by the hand and lead them to Gethsemane—to the utter loneliness of Christ as the apostles slept. There they could see Christ in his loneliness sweating blood upon a stone and, in a manner of speaking, gathering up the loneliness of the whole world as his precious blood fell upon the stone.

That is why stones are precious. Ordinary stones, in the eyes of the beholder who believes, are impregnated with drops of Christ's precious blood. Sometimes, if you touch a stone, even a little pebble, loneliness disappears—if you have faith.

Touch the Unity of the Trinity

If we wish to get rid of loneliness, we have to make contact with God, through prayer. But, there is an even deeper contact than prayer. Prayers of petition and the like are wonderful, but if we want to get rid of loneliness, we have to come closer and enter the mystery of Christ's loneliness. We must enter it without understanding it. It is impossible to understand, so, we have to make contact with God.

Consider *sobornost,* a Russian word meaning "unity." The entry into God's mysteries with the key of prayer brings us to the periphery of the *sobornost* of God the Father, Son, and Holy Spirit. This was the original *sobornost,* the original unity. We come to the periphery of this unity, and are practically in it; thus, we make a contact with it.

Having made this contact, contact with people, with my brothers and my sisters, comes naturally. My heart and your heart are so inflamed with love that they go through the world shedding love, bringing love, and putting the world on fire. That will eliminate loneliness from the lives of our brothers and sisters everywhere—and from us, too.

If we truly enter God's mystery, even at its periphery, we must love him. To him who loves God, the world is a toy to play with together with the Christ-Child.

Set the world on fire. Enter God's mystery, the unity of the Father, Son, and Holy Spirit. Let your heart be inflamed. Then, go through the world shedding love.

Touch Someone

"Let us be concerned for each other, to stir a response in love and good works. Do not absent yourself from your own assemblies, as some do, but encourage each other."

Hebrews 10:24–25

Communicate Gladly, Joyfully, Simply

The only remedy against loneliness is communication, to touch someone, not only physically but gladly, joyfully, simply, in a friendly fashion. It is quite easy, if you really love people. But, you have to love your brothers and sisters as they are.

One of the ways of dealing with loneliness, and dealing it a hard blow, is to accept people as they are. You have to love people—love them as they are, not expecting from them some performance or something extraordinary. You have to take them as they are—the people on the street or the friends that you have. You have to accept those who call themselves your friends and even your enemies.

When you accept your brother and sister as they are, friendliness toward them becomes quite normal and natural, and you can communicate with them on the level that they're at.

Communication Is Prayer

Really, there are two ways of dealing with loneliness, for when we enter the field of communication, we enter the field of sanctity. Communication incarnates the words of Christ to love one another as he loved us. When we enter the field of communication, we enter a deep and profound mystery.

One cannot truly communicate with the other except with the help of God. One must pray to the Holy Spirit, and, strangely enough, to the woman who was wrapped in silence—Mary. She did not communicate orally, but her benedictions (her way of communicating) were miraculous, because her love was almost infinite. That is why she can communicate with kings and with the lowly, when they've allowed her to. Of course, when people put up walls between the Holy Spirit or the Mother of God and themselves, then there is no communication.

I want to make this quite clear—to communicate truly with another can only be done through prayer, and powerful prayer. For this means that one loves the person he or she communicates with, and this love is of God. The Triune God can lift us to the immense heights that are required to love another as he has loved us. No fear should be attached to this act, this state of loving. If through your parents and others you have been exposed to true Christianity, then it will be easier.

Fundamentally, communication is prayer. This is difficult for people to understand. To span the distance between the casual greeting and the realm of deep, earnest, and loving prayer to him who is Love is not very easy, but it has to be done. We cannot communicate unless we love.

To communicate, one must hope as well as love. One must, also, sit under the tree of faith. Otherwise, all communication will be false and will ring falsely, as a sham, in the ears of the people we try to communicate with, and they will not respond.

If communication is really to move the heart of another person, there must be complete simplicity. Then, something happens. Suddenly, strange as it might seem, others look at us, and they see, in our humble features, the face of him who died for love of them. They catch a glimpse of something, and their hearts open. Then, we can communicate with them. The fulfillment of Christ's desire of the new commandment that he gave us, to love one another and to love our enemies, comes to full flower. The world is renewed once more, because the Lord truly smiles upon it.

Bring Christ's commandment to love one another and to love our enemies to full flower. Pray earnestly for others. Communicate with love, hope, faith— simply, joyfully, sincerely. Let Christ smile upon others through you.

> "Where there is no love, put love,
> and you will draw out love."

St. John of the Cross

Hiding Yourself

"Be servants to one another in love, since the whole of the Law is summarized in the one commandment: You must love your neighbor as yourself. If you go snapping at one another and tearing one another to pieces, take care: you will be eaten up by one another… Carry each other's burdens; that is how to keep the law of Christ."

Galatians 5:13–15; 6:2

Walking in Circles

As in Dante's circles of hell, purgatory, and heaven, we have to view loneliness as rings within our soul, and there are many.

Loneliness has many rings or circles. At times, we live in one circle, and we never wish to get out of it. It is our tranquil ring.

This is where we play the "Hi, how are you?" type of person. We realize, though, that each word that we say is totally superficial and does not communicate anything to anybody. The person constantly circles back to the point that he or she left. It is livable. One can go through life with shallow greetings and senseless questions, but if you try to love this type of person, his "Hi" interferes. This person does not want to shed his loneliness nor reveal himself. He doesn't want to communicate even with the people he's in love with or who love him.

This type of person trudges a strange circle that I would call a purgatory. It isn't a true purgatory, but it is most difficult to eternally communicate superficially, to have no friend that we can talk or share with. Such a circle is hard on people, for it is a non-sharing circle. Even to the best-loved people, the heart is not opened. Other people are not loved in the way that Christ expects people to be loved—selflessly. We circle within the self. Always, we move around to meet ourselves and start from the same point again and again.

Despair builds up. It is not complete despair, but that may come later. Still, it stays close to what it will be tomorrow or the day after. Feelingless greetings run shallow. Communication virtually doesn't exist. It may be better than nothing at all, but it is really tragic just the same. In the midst of the words that we utter, loneliness laughs at us. If loneliness could speak it would say, "You are my own. You will not escape, for you do not know how to share and communicate."

When sleep is not possible in the night, loneliness penetrates you like lightning. Then, all of the sudden, you see the sun after the storm. You look up. At that moment, you understand what it is you could be if only you overcame the lack of loving. Believe it or not, the reason why we speak so superficially is because we are hiding ourselves from people. We do not wish them to have a part in us. We want to be alone, and yet, we desperately desire friendship and understanding. Thus, loneliness holds us tight, and Dante-like rings move us between purgatory and hell.

Become Human

There are moments in the depths of night when we see, for a second, the sun shining brightly on everything, and beckoning us to come and warm ourselves in its rays. It calls us. It says, "Come! Become human. Cease to be alone. Begin to love. Begin to get involved with others. Begin to love your neighbor."

Suddenly, you understand that it is the Son who is talking to you. It is God who is calling you to get out of the morass of your loneliness.

"Reach out and touch someone," says the ad. Touch someone with the speech of your lips. Break the loneliness of others, and you will never be lonely again.

I recall one time I was in a subway in Montreal. I was reading a book when the lady across from me, who was elderly, looked at me and said, "You have a kind face. Would you mind talking to me a little? I have had the flu for the last three weeks, and only a nurse visited me for half an hour. The landlady would bring me a tray, but neither of them spoke very much. It seems I am hungry for human speech. I am hungry to share with someone. That is the way I feel."

We made two trips on the subway from one end to another. Then, I invited her to a coffee shop, and we became good friends. I did not live in Montreal, but we corresponded until she died. I hope, in fact, I know, that her loneliness had disappeared, because there was someone on the other end. There was an ear that listened lovingly. That is all we have to do.

Loneliness has many levels. You can go from one to another. You can end in a depression, for loneliness is one of the reasons for emotionally induced diseases. People leap off bridges because of loneliness. People die in nursing homes, because they've been neglected by everyone they love.

Perhaps that is why Madonna House has inaugurated listening houses. You would be very surprised—or would you—to learn that many people come to our Ottawa house just to talk. It seems that they can find no one else who listens.

Did you ever go into the nursing homes for senior citizens? There are whole floors of lonely people. Do something about it. Do something for others.

Did you ever watch the women who look through garbage cans? I wish that some photographer would take their picture and make an exhibit in a big city. They walk with their shopping bags, collecting the remnants. A series of those pictures would let us know that we have come close to an insanity created by the complete egotism and indifference of people. These are the ones that we must go to first.

It seems strange that there was a discussion going on politically between "butter and bullets". It is not a question of butter and bullets. There would be no question about bullets if the world believed in the teaching of Christ: Love your God, love your neighbor, and love your enemies.

Loneliness has many levels, many rings, many circles. One can slip deep down and become a patient in a mental institution, or one can also ascend and overcome the superficiality. One can really stop and look at his neighbour whoever he is, straight in the eye, and say, "Friend, how are you? Tell me about yourself."

Loneliness should be killed. There are three wide, beautiful roads to killing loneliness. Love your God, love your neighbor, and love your enemies.

Simple Gestures of Love

*"So always treat others
as you would like them to treat you."*

Matthew 7:12

Thrown into the Tragedy of Lust

We are prisoners today. Prisoners of so many things. Then again, are they "things" or are they states of mind? But whether things or states of mind, doesn't make any difference. We are prisoners of technology. On the horizon, appears quite clearly the domination of the machine over man. It gives a nightmarish quality of life.

For instance, large newspapers, and even small ones, offer computer dating. Even to find a mate, a person doesn't need love or anything else—one only needs a machine. In large letters the ads read, "Meet your date through a computer."

Loneliness can throw two people together in illicit, lustful embrace. Lust spells tragedy, no matter how you approach it. Machines feed and capitalize on lust. Machines keep us prisoners by exacerbating our loneliness.

Truly, we have become prisoners of technology. But this is only the beginning. Unless we smash it and become free again, freedom will cease to exist. Loneliness tears human hearts apart until they cease to be hearts.

Terrorists and Technology

Have you ever thought of or prayed for a terrorist, or for a group of them? Terrorists use all kinds of machines and are technologically equipped with bombs and explosives to kill others. They have goals, or so they think— "Liberate this or that country. Kill this man. Maim this one." But, these are the people whose nights are spent in loneliness. They have no days, only nights, because their days are as dark as night—stygian, hellish nightmares.

There is no lonelier person than a terrorist. I pray for them, because no grief can be equal to the goals terrorists set before themselves—to kill, to maim, to disrupt, to disregard men and women and children. That must be the loneliness of hell, the hell that man makes for himself. Since their cause appears to them to be viable, possible, perhaps attainable, their loneliness is doubled, for deep in their soul they know that this is not the way to peace and to love. To die for their cause appears to be beautiful, but it is monstrous because the cause itself is not beautiful.

To die for love, to die for God, to die for peace—that is beautiful, and for this we must pray.

No One Is Ordinary

Loneliness stalks every street, every dinky little alley, and every palatial home.

Juntas of every kind, trying desperately to hold on to power and wealth, still keep people imprisoned in their poverty. Those with money, barricaded with security guards, think that they are safe.

But, I do not envy the loneliness of the rich man. Nor do I envy the loneliness of a miser. I think of the Hunt brothers who at one point in their lives collared and collected the silver of the world, only to create a panic in that world. Perhaps they slept well, but I would not want to enter their loneliness.

Loneliness abides in low places and high places. But what about the ordinary people of the world? That's just it. There aren't any "ordinary" people—everyone is "extraordinary," because everyone has been created by God, and therefore, is someone to reverence.

Unfortunately, we have despised God's creation in ourselves. We have despised God's beautiful handiwork. We have despised his love, his cross, his life, the life of the second person of the Most Holy Trinity.

All this we have thrown away, as men throw away a bag of garbage. But now, we begin to wonder where we put that bag. Slowly, we have begun to understand that the remedy for the loneliness that drives us almost to suicide is hidden in that bag. We have left behind in that bag prayer, faith, love, hope, all things that used to make a person whole. They're gone. If we do not find that bag it will be tragic, because loneliness will envelop us with its unrelenting mantle. It will cover us, and although we're alive, we will be buried in the grave of loneliness, where one does not really hear or speak or understand. The black mantle of loneliness is building a grave on top of us.

Be Simple and Laugh

It is very simple—we have lost the ability to laugh, to enjoy ourselves. We have lost the joy of the simple things that were so good. The evenings with father and mother when little children were told fairy tales and went to sleep dreaming of beautiful ladies and the like. It was a time when little farms dotted the land, and most men were farmers. It was the time when children learned about trees and flowers, wheat and oats, and how they grow, when little fellows with little rakes tried to help their fathers in saving the hay. There was fun for everybody.

Everyone knew each other in the little villages and towns. There were the church suppers where everyone was friendly. There were the barn dances that disperse loneliness like wind disperses a fog. There were a thousand things that seem old but could become new any day, because they are immortal.

Communication is the enemy of loneliness. When people communicate, loneliness is broken into tiny pieces that are scattered by the wind. However, to communicate, one has to laugh.

Recently, I was in a clinic for a check up. I was astonished at the kindness and constancy of all—patients, personnel, doctors, nurses. The clinic had been built with love, sympathy, and understanding of the sick. I thought to myself, "This is what disperses loneliness." There were so many lonely people in that clinic and communication lifted it. Just a little word or a smile, a helping hand here or there, a little conversation while waiting, all these little things meant much to many people. How simple the ways of God are, how very simple!

Christ, who experienced the greatest loneliness, in a manner of speaking, gives us the power to communicate simple gestures of love—a smile, a helping hand. It is Jesus who bids us to communicate. Smile. Reach out your hand to someone.

Someone Who Understands

"I urge you, then, brothers, remembering the mercies of God, to offer your bodies as a living sacrifice, dedicated and acceptable to God; that is the kind of worship for you, as sensible people. Do not model your behaviour on the contemporary world, but let the renewing of your minds transform you, so that you may discern for yourselves what is the will of God—what is good and acceptable and mature."

Romans 12:1–2

❧

Different Kinds of Loneliness

You can go to your doctor and discuss a thousand symptoms, emotional or physical. But only a few doctors as yet seem to understand that many of the symptoms you present to their wise eyes are really the symptoms of natural, normal loneliness—the seeking of a friend, the seeking of someone who understands, of someone to cry with, someone to laugh with. Let's look a little closer at the sickness of this world called "loneliness."

There are many kinds of loneliness in the world. We do not distinguish all of them because we do not have the courage to do so. We lump them all under one word and call them "loneliness." Yet, we should differentiate.

First of all, I have learned to differentiate between solitude and loneliness. There is a vast difference between loneliness and solitude, an incredible difference between loneliness and those who choose to enter into the silence of God. These two must never be confused, because their confusion leads to more loneliness and to defiance of faith.

There is the normal loneliness that simply looks for the companionship of another human being—someone to have fun with, someone to share one's thoughts with, someone to share one's pain with. This is the normal type of loneliness. This loneliness can be eliminated, swallowed up by normal friendships.

There is the normal friendship between the young and the old that one often sees in various parks. Young people are prone to cluster around an elderly lady or gentleman who is telling them wonderful stories. There is also a friendship among peers with whom we can share the thousand things that pass through our heart, mind, and soul, year after year.

Unfortunately, today, friendship is very hard to come by. People do not make friends as they once did.

The clergy—cardinals, archbishops, bishops, and priests—also undergo a certain type of loneliness. They seek friendship just as anyone else does.

There is the kind of loneliness begotten by machines. Man needs more than machines. Because of machines, loneliness is stalking the land.

There is television, the mechanical friend, which, above all, promotes things to buy, and is probably responsible for inflation and recession. And even if it is not, in the long run, it is a monster that swallows up people wholesale. Television precludes any type of friendship except the empty greeting, "Hi how are you? Have you seen the latest program?" One returns loaded down with packages from different stores, sets them on the table, sits down, and nonetheless remains in an abysmal loneliness.

We have, also, become prisoners of computers. It will not be long before men's minds themselves will be computerized, and then, in a manner of speaking, they will cease to function normally.

We are all mixed up in this world. In our age, there is a particular kind of loneliness unknown to past generations. We don't know how to make friends. Sometimes we are almost unable to make friends. Between friendship and us lie miles and miles of electrical cords and electronic circuits.

There was a time (older people can tell you), when people were neighbors. They did not sit glaring at television with glassy stares.

No, people were neighbors. They used to visit each other, or play games together or other kinds of entertainment.

One of the most terrible sights that anyone can behold is that of old people living on a meager pension. It is barely enough to feed them. Slowly, they decline into an abysmal state of loneliness. During their last years, none of their children come to visit them.

One can see how loneliness eats them up, as cancer does. This kind of loneliness is prevalent all over the world, especially the western world.

Do Something to Open Your Soul

There was a time when people painted, wrote books, and opened their souls in thousands of ways to others. People could talk and think together. One could read a book, see a picture, view a display or an exhibition. Today we can still see an exhibition or read a book—that is still possible—although very soon books may be read only through electronic recordings, and there will be nothing left.

There are all kinds of loneliness. Loneliness is almost a part of us. We cry for release to a heaven that at times we even refuse to believe in. Someday we will understand that we have become prisoners of computers. Someday, we will arise and destroy their fascinating power, and we will be free again; we will be able to communicate with others. Someday, our loneliness will disappear.

There might be people who are lonelier than I ever was or ever will be, but I understand loneliness. How many of you feel the desire to write to me? I know that many do, because I have fallen in love with mankind—men, women, children. All of humanity is dear to my heart.

Everyone must bear his or her cross of loneliness. Friend, I love you. You know I do, and, even if you never write to me, remember that there is someone who really loves you, and, strangely enough, understands you.

"As far as I am concerned, the greatest suffering is to feel alone, unwanted, unloved."
Mother Teresa

Expressing Tenderness to Another

"Keep your minds calm and sober for prayer. Above all preserve an intense love for each other, since love covers over many a sin. Welcome each other into your houses without grumbling. Each one of you has received a special grace… put it at the service of others."

1 Peter 4:7–10

Offer a Tender Touch

We talk much about loneliness, for loneliness is a most terrible thing.

There are two kinds of loneliness—one is human loneliness and the other is divine loneliness.

"My heart will not rest until it rest in Thee." (St. Augustine) That is divine loneliness. That is the loneliness of the person to whom Christ said, "Follow me."

There is another loneliness that is human. It is painful, tears you apart, sometimes blurring the face of the loneliness that Christ sends us. It is a terrible thing, and we must do something about. It is here that tenderness, gentleness, and understanding help us to live in both lonelinesses, but especially the human—the ordinary one. Gentleness and tenderness assuage loneliness and make it possible to disappear.

Many people who have read many spiritual books (and those who have not) think tenderness is sort of a feminine virtue exhibited by mothers toward their children. But, if a marriage doesn't include tenderness, only passion and sex, it will not last very long.

Tenderness is the ability to be present, extending the warmth of my heart to your heart. It is an unspoken thing. It can, of course, be expressed, with great difficulty. Few people have this ability to express tenderness in a spoken way. But all people can express tenderness by a glance, or by putting a hand on someone. That person will feel the warmth that comes from another.

Go Deeper

When people say, "I want to be loved," they usually mean that they want to be loved by a person who belongs to them. Some seek love in marriage. I need not talk to you about this, because you come to Madonna House from a thousand broken homes, not all of you but many of you. When we look around Canada and the U.S., what do we see? Millions of broken homes. The reason for the hippies was broken homes. Alcoholism is the result of broken homes in many ways. Name the tragedy of youth, and you find it in the home.

These gifts, these virtues of tenderness, gentleness, and understanding are so simple, so everyday that we really forget about them. We are either harsh on ourselves or harsh on others. Oh, not completely, because we are polite people.

But if I reject someone in my heart, because she is fat or thin, because of likes or dislikes, if I reject one human being in my heart, I add to the cross of loneliness of that person. Whether you know it or not, a heavy burden of rejection falls on their shoulders, which are already burdened. I speak exclusively of a rejection that nobody knows about. The other person doesn't feel it officially, because you and I can be very polite and decent. But it is in the depth of the heart.

There is some kind of a strange recompense. The good that we do goes across the world and probably into the cosmos. The evil that we do follows the same path. It is rather fearsome isn't it?

Always go deeper. Find out what is in the heart. Get the crab grass that can cover the heart faster than it can pull this crab grass out. Weed your heart from all those things.

When God Is Forgotten

I was reading a very strange book about suicides. The highest rates of suicide are in Sweden, Denmark, and Norway.

Sweden is a very wonderful country. It is highly civilized, very technological. Why do they kill themselves? They have forgotten God.

Not to be close to God, not to make a community with the Trinity, (which is the first and eternal community), is to create an atmosphere that is prevalent in Sweden. It will become prevalent in us if we forget what it is all about. We better remember, or our loneliness will reach impossible degrees.

To love one another means to bring joy and peace, gentleness, tenderness, and understanding. All these things into one, and offer it to your brother or sister. Hospitality is one way of abolishing the loneliness of others. It is gentle, tender, merciful, and understanding to others.

Treat Yourself with Gentleness

The Lord is tenderness and pity,
slow to anger and rich in faithful love;
his indignation does not last for ever,
nor his resentment remain for all time;
he does not treat us as our sins deserve,
nor repay us as befits our offences.
As the height of heaven above the earth,
so strong is his faithful love for those who fear him.
As the distance of east from west,
so far from us does he put our faults.
As tenderly as a father treats his children,
so the Lord treats those who fear him.

Psalm 103:8–13

Gentleness, with Compassion and Understanding

I ask myself, "What is this marvelous gift of the Holy Spirit which allows us to see into the heart of another?" It is discernment of our own heart.

The gift of discernment, the gift of listening, the gift of being quiet in your heart, it is in the quiet of your heart where discernment lies.

It is very difficult to apply to oneself. So many people come to Madonna House with a strange question. Or is it a strange question? They ask, "What is my vocation? How do I know my vocation?"

Let us not narrow the meaning of the word "vocation." Don't narrow it down to religious life only. Vocation is a state of life in a sense, but the broad and wide understanding of vocation is very simple. A vocation is a call of God to love him back in a state of priestly life, religious life, married life, single life, any kind of life. We all have vocations, spiritually speaking. We all have the vocation to love God back, because he loved us first.

To approach discernment you have to walk *gently*. You have to be full of *compassion* and certainly pray to God for the gift of *understanding*, both of yourself and others. We are so quick to be un-gentle, un-tender, un-understanding with each other, and so quick with self-pity.

Self-Pity Makes You Blind and Deaf

Self-pity is a deadly thing. It kills all understanding, because once I wrap myself up in the mantle of self-pity, I am blind and deaf as portrayed in the gospel.

We are very rough on ourselves sometimes. The fact that we wrap ourselves up in self-pity doesn't mean that we don't wrap ourselves up in the mantle of eternal guilt, too. So between self-pity and guilt, we balance ourselves like a girl on the flying trapeze and we don't get anywhere. We keep on flying never being able to come down to the real hard-brass tacks of God and his ways.

To be gentle with oneself is to express what God does to me daily. It is to express his mercy, his truth. We are sinners, but don't forget the word "saved" before you call yourself a sinner. We are *saved sinners*. God saved us, brought us back to his Father, so be gentle in facing yourself. We can very easily say to ourselves, "Now, wait a minute.

Don't get into all this emotional and unemotional and spiritual business about guilt." No. Don't do that. Be gentle with yourself, for God is gentle with you.

If you know that you have committed a sin, (or something has happened that you are sorry for), if it is necessary, go to confession and you will have peace. But please forget about it. If God has forgiven you, why should you remember?

Gentleness to oneself will beget gentleness toward others. Always hold on to the gentleness of God.

On Gentleness to Ourselves

"One form of gentleness we should practice is towards ourselves. We should never get irritable with ourselves because of our imperfections. It is reasonable to be displeased and sorry when we commit faults, but not fretful or spiteful to ourselves...

"All irritation with ourselves tends to foster pride and springs from self-love, which is displeased at finding we are not perfect.

"We should regard our faults with calm, collected, and firm displeasure. We correct ourselves better by a quiet persevering repentance than by an irritated, hasty, and passionate one.

"When your heart has fallen raise it gently, humbling yourself before God, acknowledging your fault, but not surprised at your fall. Infirmity is infirm, weakness weak, and frailty frail."

St. Francis de Sales

A Miracle

Jesus [said], "Everything is possible for one who has faith." At once the father of the boy cried out, "I have faith. Help my lack of faith!"

Mark 9:24

Make the Journey

Once, I studied psychiatry. The doctor that taught me was called Armstrong. He was an atheist, but kind of a kind atheist.

He was very punctilious in telling nurses that the best psychological approach in counseling was in the confessional. The Catholic Church had a secret of counseling. He spoke of it in a secular way.

One day I took my courage in both hands and said, "Doctor, why don't you go to Lourdes? You are a single man. You are middle-aged. You have no family. It would be for you an experience. A psychological, psychiatric experience." I put it on thick. I challenged him a little.

He said, "I have nothing to do next vacation time. I'll do that little thing."

He wrote to Lourdes. He eventually got permission to get on the board.

When you become a doctor at Lourdes for a certain spell, you are allotted some patients. Lourdes does not accept psychological cures. They must be physical. So he was allotted a TB patient.

She had TB of the bone. It was such bad TB that you could see the bone, for the flesh had been eaten up. She weighed practically nothing. The orderly and nurse gave him all the x-rays and all the information.

It was a miracle she arrived from wherever she was from—Switzerland, I think.

He was there to meet her. From the moment she arrived, he was supposed to follow her and he did.

Pray for Faith

He told us all this when he returned. He said, "I walked around these places where they dipped those people in. It was a very cold flow. They dipped those people in one right after another. My doctor's heart practically turned upside-down because one person after another with boils and what not! The water should be contaminated.

"Came the time for my patient to come there. I shivered. There was nothing I could do. She wanted to get in there. They wanted her to get in there. What could I do? So I said to myself, 'Okay, if she gets cured I'll become a Catholic. There are no two ways about it. It will never happen.'

"Three times she was dipped into it. She fainted but she came to on the third time. I examined the leg. There was no wound. There was nothing. Just a perfectly healed leg. I couldn't even know where the thing was if I hadn't seen it before.

"You know," he said, "I'm not ashamed to say that right there in the midst of all those places where they bathe, I fell on my knees. I was struck like lightening. There she was. One moment she had a wound. The next moment she had nothing. The next moment she got up, thin as she was, weak as she was, and this was proclaimed a healing. I had to sign all this. There were about eleven doctors besides myself who read through all her x-rays and all that. I came out of there and said, 'Lead me to a Catholic priest.' "

And he came back to the hospital I trained in, from an atheist to a Catholic. This is a miracle of God.

But you see, the footprints. The bloody footprints, the harsh and impossible, and terrible love of God. The girl suffered for so long. Perhaps she was there just to bring one man back to God. Think of her joy after the suffering. Think of his joy. What appears a harsh and terrible love is really not at all any more. It really is gentle, beautiful, tender love, patient love, constant love, unfailing.

It's something for us to think about today for we are very much tempted to abandon our ideas. "Oh, Gosh, I've been in this movement so long and the community so long. I've been here and there, and nothing happens, nothing happens, and I want to quit."

Or, like some who visit us say, "All is well in Madonna House, but when I go out, it will be different."

But did you ever stop to think how much went into Madonna House? How many of the staff here were very much like the lady with the TB. They didn't have TB but they

too had doubts. They too had difficulties.
They too had problems, and they still have
them, and their answer is prayer. Prayer for
faith, not just prayer to get away from their
problem.

*You face the problem you accept the problem, but
you pray for faith. Because faith becomes luminous
as you pray for it. It shines upon this kind of a situa-
tion and allows you to really believe what God
wants you to believe. As you grow in faith you
become shiny—I mean shiny from within with a sort
of strange hidden shininess. Then, people come to
you, not knowing why, and you don't know why, but
they come. They come, and they get healed, not by
you but by the faith in God that made you bring him
closer to the other. When this happens, when faith is
growing, when prayer brings it near you, then, in the
hearts of many, there is a strange joy, a happiness
that they didn't think could be theirs.*

God's Love is Harsh

"Of course, any discipline is at the time a matter for grief, not joy; but later, in those who have undergone it, it bears fruit in peace and uprightness. So steady all weary hands and trembling knees and make your crooked paths straight; then the injured limb will not be maimed, it will get better instead."

Hebrews 12:11–13

Surrender

One of the things that sometimes comes to you when you think of God is his strangeness. We're human. We tend to project our humanness onto God. (Of course, God is human, too—the second person of the Trinity). We tend to project things onto him, but he doesn't like being projected onto, because he is himself.

One of the things that hits you when you pray is a sort of complexity—in simplicity, because God is simple. Look at this. God loves us. He loved us first. He died for us. All beautiful stuff. He is compassionate. He is tender. He is full of mercy. Yet his love is inexorable. His love is harsh. His love seems almost cruel; certainly, it is *"terribilis"*[5]—it's terrible.

How will you reconcile in your heart this compassion, this tenderness, this love, this harshness, and this almost terror—*terribilis?* It's not easy. It's the way of man to God laid out by God. The only thing that helps you to reconcile it is the fact the he walked that road and that you have footsteps to walk into.

After you walk in his footsteps, you will understand that he loves us with a *passionate* love. Not just a love that we sort of conceive ourselves. No, he loves us with a love so passionate, so complete, so total, that he desires, above all, our happiness. He knows. He knows because he is God that the only happiness is to walk in his footsteps.

We look at them. We say, "No! But they are bloody! I don't want to walk in bloody footsteps. That means pain. That means something of surrender. I want to walk to

5   "Terribilis" is the Latin root of "terrible."

the left and to the right and wherever I want to walk."[6]

The footsteps are clear, shining in the night of faith, shining in the day of doubt, shining at all times. Even when we try to run away and say, "To heck with the Church. To heck with everything. I don't buy this stuff!" the shiny footsteps are before our eyes. As Francis Thompson, an English poet, wrote, "He followed me across the arches of the years."

Walk in the Footprints

So we are confronted within ourselves. Especially, as we pray, we are confronted within ourselves with this choice. To us, it is a terrible choice, because we do not know. We do not know that the moment we put our foot into that bloody footprint we will know *joy* beyond understanding. The joy that he promised us. *Peace* beyond understanding that he promised us. It takes an act

---

6 "Only be strong and stand very firm and be careful to keep the whole Law which my servant Moses laid down for you. Do not swerve from this either to right or to left, and then you will succeed wherever you go." (Joshua 1:7)

of will and especially an act of faith to be able to walk into those footsteps, and to believe, believe against every reason, against everything that is in front of us, that to walk in those footsteps is joy and will give us peace.

This is the struggle today. Man decides that peace and joy and everything else that they think is really happiness lies somewhere else, not in those footprints. Somewhere else. So people wander and wander, like in a circle. And where do they come to? No place. They come in a circle right back to where they left, spent and tired, still doubting. At least, they come back knowing by experience that these circles that they thought were happiness, prosperity, and money, and whatever is supposed to be happiness for each, are like sawdust in the mouth.

Pray

Once more we cast our minds into the seeking of peace, into the desire for joy to be found in God. We begin to pray. Praying is an excruciating thing. Our mind wanders hither, thither, and yon, like a thousand flies. Rather than emptying itself, our head buzzes with ideas.

Gradually, we understand the harshness of the Lord. He becomes our physician. Have you ever looked at an operation? If you didn't understand what was going on you'd say, "My God, look at the harshness of that surgeon. Look at the things that he is using, saws to cut open the head or cut off a limb." It looks like a torture chamber to an uninitiated one. But the Divine Physician appearing harsh is not harsh. He is healing—healing as no doctor can, for he can make all wounds new.

If you have a wound, Jesus, the Divine Physician, can touch it, and the flesh will become as if it never had a wound.

Restoration

Jesus exclaimed, "I bless you, Father, Lord of heaven and of earth, for hiding these things from the learned and the clever and revealing them to little children."…

"Come to me, all who labour and are overburdened, and I will give you rest. Shoulder my yoke and learn from me, for I am gentle and humble in heart, and you will find rest for your souls. *Yes, my yoke is easy and my burden light."*

Matthew 11:25, 28–30

God Makes Us New

Those of us who possess creative talents of any kind must really go in depth.

Take for instance Fr. Lenius. I have often looked at him and my meditation on loneliness gets deeper and deeper. He has a talent of restoring old furniture.

He does very simple things. Although he uses the implements of restoration, whatever they may be, there is something in his hands, something in himself, something in his heart that loves the wood, that does something to it that is beyond what an ordinary person would do for money. He is an artist of restoration. Today the world calls it "recycling". I like the word "restoration" better.

He restored an old-fashioned, 1850 or something, sewing machine—a cabinet—and I thought of the beauty of the thing. As it came forth, it glowed, it was new, and yet it had the vulnerability of old.

To restore, to make new, is part of creation. That is what God does—he constantly restores us, constantly makes us new.

Awaken the Power to Create Beauty

The loneliness—the face that comes from God, is something that we should meditate on deeply and profoundly, because in it lies the answer to our modern world.

Consider the strange loneliness that comes from God so that we may awaken to the power within us—to our neglected ability to make things new—or to create from clay or something, beauty. The Lord loves beauty. His world was beautiful until we messed it up, but it is still beautiful in spots.

If Father Lenius can restore a machine to its beauty that is over a hundred years old, maybe we can accept the loneliness of God. Accept the loneliness to walk alone with God because that is his invitation.

He says, "Yes you need help from other people but first get me. Attach yourself to me. I will give you everything else, for I am the Lord of everything. I will give it to you renewed, restored, and you yourself will have new eyes and new ears. Enter the loneliness of faith, enter the loneliness, and you will be a new person. You will be new, because you will hear the voice simultaneously—my voice and that of men for whom I died. You will see into the hearts of men and bring them to me."

"Be attentive, O souls that I love,
to the sufferings of My Heart."

Servant of God Sister Josefa Menéndez
(private revelation)[7]

7   Nihil Obstat: Patricius Morris, S.T.D., L.S.S., Censor Deputatus. Imprimatur: X E. Morrogh Bernard, Vic. Gen.,

You Belong to God

*"We are God's work of art, created in Christ Jesus
for the good works which God has already
designated to make up our way of life."*

Ephesians 2:10

The Hunger to Lead People to God

The land of loneliness is the land of joy, the land of union with God, the land of hunger for God, the land of understanding that God alone matters. The land of loneliness is a fantastic place that words cannot describe. It is the land of belonging to God.

I think the secret of that land is that the hunger for God grows like a fire. In fact, it is a fire. At the same time, the love of humanity intensifies itself and there is only one thought in the land of loneliness—to lead men to God.

Westmonasterii, die 5a Maii, 1953.

I think that's why it's called the "land of loneliness." There is only one thought, one goal, one dream that matters and that is leading people to God. It's a passion. It's the only desire, but people do not go to God. That is why it is the land of loneliness. I think that's the loneliness that Christ experienced before death, during his whole life probably, but intensely in the Garden of Gethsemane.

To lead men to God, that is the land of loneliness. To know a little bit of who God is, to passionately desire to give him to men—all men and women and children—humanity, to try to give him to the best of one's ability, and then to find that people do not want to accept him in total. They want only to give him a token of themselves, a quarter, maybe, but not all. So one walks the land of loneliness. In that land there is no possibility of manipulating other people. It can't be done, because God won't allow it any more.

However, God will manipulate. The weight of God is heavy even in this land, especially, in the land of loneliness. The one who walks in the land of loneliness is on his way to being able to say, "I live not. Christ lives in me."

A Heart Opening to God

How all of us need each other in a different way than God wants us to need each other!

To enter into that land of loneliness, all my needs, anybody's needs, must be centered on God alone. They are there, the needs. They don't fall away. Some of them do but not all. The need for many things is still there but that is the tunic, the only tunic that the pilgrim who enters the land of loneliness wears. At times, it looks like a hairshirt, but at times, it's downy and soft.

It seems to me that one of the fruits of the land of loneliness will be the repossession of everyone by everyone in Christ. The need for approval, the need for feeling needed, the need for directing other people toward God or one's own intellect, brilliancy or what-have-you will fall away. I think that eventually, I don't know because I've barely entered that land, but I think that friendship becomes simple and joyous, that all needs being centered in Christ and the blazing desire to bring people to God softens all things, even the fact that I do not count on doing any of those things.

The land of loneliness is a human heart opening itself to the possession by God, as far as human hearts understand total possession. One understands that without him one can do nothing. It reduces one's self, at first, to a sort of zero, a non-entity, until the wings of the intellect fold and the heart opens, and the intellect is illuminated by Christ. Then, one understands a little bit better the words of Teresa of Avila: "I and a ducat are nothing, but I and a ducat and God is everything." And here her sentences can be paraphrased: I cannot lead anyone anywhere, by myself, but if I allow myself to be filled with God, I can lead men to God.

So the land of loneliness is the land of intense peace and a strange joy. But God does not yet allow loneliness to be eliminated from peace and joy. That will come after death.

I don't know, but I think that along the road to God that started in baptism, confirmation, and Eucharist, through a Christian life of contemplation, moving toward union with him, the land of loneliness is the last step before total union with God. But I am convinced that the land of loneliness is not, for everyone, something that comes just before death. For many people, it will come in their early youth, middle age, at any time their hearts are open to it, if they love enough and if God desires it to be so.

※

God alone matters. Hunger for God. Belong to God. Give everyone to God and God to everyone.

Holiness

"Seek peace *with all people, and the holiness without which no one can ever see the Lord. Be careful that no one is deprived of the grace of God and that no* root of bitterness should begin to grow and make trouble; *this can poison a large number....* What you have come to is nothing known to the senses."

Hebrews 12:14–15, 18

The Hunger for Holiness

The loneliness of God is a creative loneliness.

Priests especially should think about that for they are the loneliest people on earth if you want to look on it from a human point of view—because we love them, because generations of people have loved them, because we have put them on a pedestal, not for themselves but for what they say or do—

the Christ in them—because we understand that without them the heat of our day may be so intense that we may perish, for without the bread, without the wine, how shall we walk the road of Christ? If it is just impossible to have a priest, Christ will be the priest, but when the priest is there he has to give us the means, the strength to walk in that darkness of faith. What about him? He has been set apart and rightly or wrongly, relegated to his presbytery or to his monastery.

Things have developed. You know humanity is always going out in a hurry someplace so you cannot blame God for something humanity has done but the totality of the result of what humanity has done in the past hundred years or more is that the priests are the loneliest people in the Latin Rite, and don't get the idea either that the priests of the Eastern Rite who marry are less lonely.

Loneliness, or the loneliness of God, has nothing to do with being single or married, old or young. It is something quite different. There is no one who loves God who is exempt from his loneliness, because it is one of the deepest ways by which God calls a person to share his loneliness, and in sharing his loneliness, to become what he really is—a creative restorer—one who brings beauty and new life to his fellow man.

What are we all hungering for? Let us use that word—"holiness"—that is what we are hungering for—*holiness*. What is holiness? Holiness is the forgetfulness of oneself for others. Deep down in our hearts all of us wish we could really be holy. The way to holiness is loneliness.

Have Mercy!

Inevitably those of mankind who try to fall in love with God, or are in love with God, will experience the point of crying out, almost howling in the face of God, "Have mercy. Do something." Strangely enough he will do nothing because he wants that faith to awaken that person to move toward him, and once we face the loneliness of God, its creativeness, the restoration of ourselves and others that comes with it, we begin to understand that it is not a loneliness at all because at some point he reveals himself and says in so many words, without speaking, "I was with you all the time."

If God is with us there can be no loneliness. In that restoration, that renewal we accomplish through him, he shows us what he has done for us, because we have followed his call, we have accepted that loneliness.

The loneliness of a priest is a gift to me. Here is a priest in the midst of a busy place like Toronto, New York, Chicago. Here he sits and has a little self-pity maybe or what-have-you, or has not thought through whether the loneliness is from himself or God. Once he comprehends that it is from God, strange things happen around him— the parish, the people, rally.

There was in Harlem a man like that, a 6-foot-4, redheaded Irishman, Father Michael Mulvoy. He loved the Negro. He was ahead of his time about 50 years. He started all kinds of things for the Negro.

He used to come to Friendship House. And he would sit in front of me in the library and say, "Catherine, do you know how lonely a priest can get?" Well, I am not a priest, but I can tell you how lonely a woman can get. Then, we would sit in front of each other and say nothing because there was nothing to say. But I knew he probed my loneliness, and I probed his.

The strange thing about Father Mulvoy was that when his superiors (he was a Holy Ghost Father) sent him to Alabama to a white university because he had become a little too prominent in Harlem, he was so much loved that the Communist Party people went to Cardinal Spellman and begged Cardinal Spellman to keep him there. I am not speaking of the fact that Protestants, Catholics, atheists, Negroes went, but white and Negro communist members went to beg for him and said, "We did not believe in the Nazarene but when we see Father Mulvoy we begin to believe in the Nazarene." Now that is a tribute! He was alienated from his priests, from his superiors, everybody, but this terrible loneliness did something to the people. They did not understand it, but felt it, because out of his loneliness came a creativity that helped the rest of the people.

When you discuss loneliness and come to think about it, think about the loneliness of Christ, of God—the loneliness that God gave us to bring us to himself.

Afterword

We have been discussing loneliness. And yet, if we think of it, we really have not discussed anything because one cannot discuss loneliness. The only way we could discuss loneliness is if we could enter Christ's loneliness.

My mind turns toward obedience. Here is God, the second person of the Most Holy Trinity. The Father sends him down to redeem us. And, without a murmur, he enters as a seed into a woman's womb. How did he do it? He was God. I know that many heresies arose regarding that point, and many people argued about it. I do not argue, and I am not interested in heresy. I just behold the humility of Christ. I behold the love of Christ, for only lovers can do such things.

Those of us who were baptized in his name are his body, the people of God. He is our head. This is good theology. But there is here a tremendous mystery. It is as if I approach slowly, barefoot, towards this mystery, shining in the distance. Then, I stop, because it is one of the incomprehensible

mysteries. The only way man could understand this mystery, embrace it, is if man
loved God as God loves him. Then, and only
then, the mystery of the redemption is
revealed. What is the mystery of the redemption? It is the mystery of the passionate love
of God for man.

So then, man must seek to love God the
same way that God loves him. This is what
Christ said we should do: "I give you a new
commandment: love one another; you must
love one another just as I have loved you."
Thus, we stand in front of this mystery.
Suddenly, he takes us by the hand and says,
"Come." Then, as we move into this mystery,
the mystery of love opens before us, the
mystery of surrender to the cross, the mystery of the resurrection.

True, there is always his passionate love
of his Church. True, the Church has other
mysteries. True, it is the bride of Christ, and
if you want to probe loneliness, that is where
you have to enter. You have to penetrate the
mystery of Christ becoming man, and then
you will know what loneliness is. It will
frighten you and you will try to run from it,
but stay. Keep moving *into* the mystery. As
you move in, as the door of love, the door of

surrender, the door of obedience, and the door of passionate loving opens, something will happen to you. Your loneliness will completely change.

I do not care if you have the most beloved husband or wife in the world. It makes no difference if you are a nun or a priest who is completely lost in love with God. You will always know the incredible longing for the unity of man in God.

At some point, maybe in your youth, maybe in your old age, maybe in your middle age—you will suddenly feel that your lifted hands, which were praying to God and fasting, will slowly come down, and, instead of lying as usual by your side, they will come down, and loneliness will disappear. You cannot even imagine loneliness, then, because your hands have finally reached the hands of Christ.

Then, there will remain only one thing. He will bend down his face, and, as it says in Song of Songs, he will kiss you on the lips. You will look around, and there will be no loneliness. Death makes loneliness disappear forever. Not only will faith and hope fall away, but loneliness will fall away.

However, we have to live in this world until death comes to fetch us. Since God has invited you to come into this mystery of his loneliness, since you have probed it, tasted it, felt it, since your hands and feet have the sign of nails, since you have explored his love for his Church—the Bride—since those things have happened to you, do not think for a moment that they are there just for you. No! They are there for everyone. Now, at long last, your hands are in the hands of Christ. But before your lips touch his, you have to assuage the loneliness of others who have not moved into the mystery of God's loneliness.

Now, you have one great work of God's mercy to perform: Go and assuage loneliness. Make those people who think they are alone understand that no one is ever alone, because everyone is with Christ. Go, for the time is ripe. The whole earth is lonely. Go forth, and chase away the loneliness.

Books by Catherine Doherty

In the Footprints of Loneliness
In the Furnace of Doubts
On the Cross of Rejection

Madonna House Classics

Poustinia: Encountering God in Silence,
Solitude and Prayer
Sobornost: Unity of Mind, Heart and
Soul
Strannik: The Call to the Pilgrimage of
the Heart
Molchanie: The Silence of God
Uródivoi: Holy Fools
Bogoroditza: She Who Gave Birth to God

Available in electronic format at
www.madonnahouse.org/publications

Audio Books

Fragments of My Life
Not Without Parables
Poustinia
Sobornost
Strannik

MADONNA HOUSE PUBLICATIONS

COMBERMERE • ONTARIO • CANADA • KOJ 1L0

The aim of our publications is to share the Gospel of Jesus Christ with all people from all walks of life.

It is to awaken and deepen in our readers an experience of God's love in the most simple and ordinary facets of everyday life.

It is to make known to our readers how to live the tender, saving life of God in everything they do and for everyone they meet.

Our publications are dedicated to Our Lady of Combermere, the Mother of Jesus and of His Church, and we are under her protection and care.

Madonna House Publications is a non-profit apostolate of Madonna House within the Catholic Church. Donations allow us to send books to people who cannot afford them but most need them all around the world. Thank you for your participation in this apostolate.

To request a catalogue of our current publications, please call (613) 756-3728, or write to us at:

Madonna House Publications
2888 Dafoe Rd, RR 2
Combermere ON K0J 1L0
Canada

All of our publications are available on our website:

www.madonnahouse.org/publications